ANDREW HAWES
COLLECTED POEMS
1970 - 2014

To she who is my flesh;
To those who share my flesh;
And those
with whom I partake
His flesh.

ANDREW HAWES
COLLECTED POEMS
1970 – 2014

Edited by
Andrew Berry

Foreword by
Patrick Hawes

HAWES MUSIC
PUBLISHING

HAWES MUSIC PUBLISHING

The Rectory, Catfield, Norfolk NR29 5DB

First edition published in 2014 by Hawes Music Ltd.

ISBN 978-1-910623-02-2

A catalogue record for this publication is available from the British Library.

Printed and bound in England by
Caligraving Ltd, Thetford, Norfolk

CONTENTS

CHRISTMAS POEMS

FOREWORD

Some siblings are as different as chalk and cheese. This is definitely not the case, however, with my brother and me. Since our earliest years, we seem to have seen the world through similar eyes and have grown up holding the same core beliefs. Much of this must be to do with our upbringing - the sons of honest, hardworking parents who instilled in us both the desire to strive for the best in all things while maintaining a sense of humour and, above all, never harming others. Our grandparents had their influence too: they were dear people who fought for every penny they earned and put their family before anything else.

It is no wonder, then, that 'family' is a strong theme in Andrew's poetry. His wife Siân and my five nephews and nieces all make their appearance, and the backdrop of the family home is there as well. The Queen Anne vicarage in Edenham is where most of this poetry has been written, and the reader can frequently feel the presence of the strong tower of the church of St. Michael and All Angels which stands only yards away from the building where Andrew and his family have lived and worked.

The thing I understand most about my brother, though, is his faith. I share that faith and feel its nuances in the same way. I believe with all my heart that Andrew's faith is special - quite unlike that of countless other priests I have met. In one way, it is unfortunate that he has lived through a time of such fundamental change in the Anglican Church and found himself alienated and sidelined. Had the Church into which he was baptised, confirmed and ordained been as loyal to him as he has been to the Church, then his Christian teachings would have reached a much wider cross-section of people. It may be, though, that he would not have written so much poetry. Pen and paper have been his solace as much as they have been the means of capturing moments of joy and fulfilment. As with every note of my music, every word he writes is an offering to God. In 1989, the poems he wrote for *The Wedding at Cana* moved me to tears as I set them, and the words I have clothed in music since then are imprinted on my soul. I know many of the poems in this book by heart. I have 'lived' them and diffused them into musical sound, and I am much the better person as a result. It is my hope that all those who read the poems in this collection will be moved, even changed, in a similar way.

PATRICK HAWES
2014

THE COLLECTED POEMS
1970 - 2014
OF
ANDREW HAWES

THE BEACH IN WINTER

The road to the beach lay white
Untrod.
No little children clamber to the sea's
entrancing roar.
The sand dunes
Sit bleak, flamboyant
Against a white-washed sky.
The sea
Grey
Forbidding
Crashes
Upon the
Helpless sand.

1970

EMPTINESS TO EMPTINESS

Emptiness rolls on –
Lives
Begin and end.
Punctuating like clouds (the sky)
That from nothing
Swell
Emerge
Grow heavy full
Then empty
On others
Sorrow
      Happiness.
Like leaves
We come to follow
To protect
To feed, to live upon
The naked
Bare
Tree.
We grow
Sway
Colourful;
To wither
Shrivel
Die
And fall
To become nothing.

1971

WITH THE TIDE

The yellow lamps arcing
The clear-frost night
Black as witches
The beat and click of
Footwear on the path
Hurrying home to slippers
And the six o'clock news.

Bumper to bumper
Exhaust grey clouds
Spill into the night
The light-tide
Full-beam ploughs
Home in earnestness.

And alone at the
Corner I cross the road.

1973

SHEFFIELD 1974-77

I love those streets
The ones that frame
The pennine sky;
Those grey streets
Those glistening streets
Of chunky slate and stone.

Our street was a
Long one,
Up and down hill,
Truncated
By the traffic lights
That always looked
So bright.

Round the corner is
The post office;
It always smelt
Of wet dogs
And warm paraffin.

And
There always
Seemed to be
Dustbins
Scattered about,
With numbers
In emulsion on.

That street was
Magic though
And I remember
In the snow
It turned into
The cresta run.

With beer warm
Heads
We hooted down
The road,
The whole
Affair
Was street lamp lit
In ghostly yellow.

In the summer
The smell of dust
And all the
Bouncing
Scant clad girls
And
Exams.

Staring at
The passersby
Unseen
Through dirty nets;
The room became
A welcome pile
Of books
And empty
Bottles.

I remember.
It was always
Dark inside. But,
Cosy
All the same.

1977

FAIRACRES (1)

I felt as if
I'd stumbled
Into a
Darkened room
Where
Lovers
Silently caressed.

Yet,
They were not ashamed,
But lingered
There;
Not afraid
To look
Me in the eye.

1977

FAIRACRES (2)

Eucharist.

Ticking clocks
And endless
Echoes
Of time
In chiming
Bells
Singing
Out the visits
Of eternity.

Clocks
In every room
Just
Tick
To prove
That time
Is only
Sanctified
In seconds.

1977

8

HYACINTH

I bought them
In a string bag
On a little spree
One weekday

They hung in the pantry
All brown and flaky
As the nights drew in.

When it was too late:
When all the Christmas cake
Had gone,
I rammed them in a bowl.

And they began to grow
Dry and twisting
From their tips.

And now I wait
To see
If they will bloom
In Lent.

1978

9

THE CHAMPION OF THE THAMES

Mid-day
And deadly sloth
Strikes,
Nodding by the gas fire
And it's bleak outside.

Pull on
The coat
Feeling in pockets,
Checking for keys
"We're off." says I,
And slam the door.

Across the road
Hop up the steps,
Whistling in a windy kind of way,
Dodging through
The flats –
The one with grape
Vines so rich in summer
Gone all withered and black.

Duck down an alley
And there's 'The Champ'.
Open the door
And walk into
The smoke.

"Alright?"
"Alright."
"A pint please Les."
"Cold?" says he
"Aye." says I.

Slouch in the corner
By the fuming stove.

Timeless
Changeless
They're all
Still sitting there.

The old lady
Nags her husband in
Strident fenland tones;
He nods his cap
And studies form

Then in they walk:
Two strangers.
Eyes move over glasses.

"Hello Les,"
Les goes red.
"Remember me?"
"I think I do –
Used to drink with Joseph"

"Right."
Says he.
The pale-faced girl
Buys his pint
And they sit down.

They roll their own.

She spoke nicely
And wore a tatty fur.
He was loud and
Had long straggly hair.

They mouthed across the room
To everyone around,
And I shuffled embarrassed
In my corner of the room.

But they just soaked them up.

1978

12

ON READING GEORGE MELLY'S "OWNING UP"

Da-da
And all that
Was you
And you
Did live
Out Dali's
Living scape.

Your world
Became a
World of
Booze and blues
And you made
The tune of
Slaves
Your livelihood.

In outworn
Tones you
Drank a
Deeper draught
Of music
And a language
Not your own.

You threw
Your body
On the pile
Of lust.

You travelled
Home-on-back
With others:
Hunting like
A pack

In search of
Homelessness
And tears.

And yet it
Seems above
All else
To me you sought
Your tingling
Life because
You knew
That someone
Somewhere
Cares.

1978

PLUS KEN AT LAST

At last
We snapped the case
And I was on
My way.

At last
I droned through black
Then glinted
Over
The cold blue gulf.

At last
I wandered
Through the smell
Of dawn
At Bahrain airport.

At last
I crossed
The blotched out
Worn out
Brown
Of India.

At last
I saw
The luscious clouds
That kiss
Sumatra.

At last
I saw the
Teeming light
Of Singapore
And glided
Silent
Into its heart.

At last
The man
Said
To me
We are to land
In Darwin.

At last
He told
Me the
Price of taxis
And ways to
The esplanade.

At last
I saw
Tiny
White lights
Speckled round
The sea.

At last
I scuttled
From the belly
Of the plane
And stood
And sweated
In the queue
And breathed
Beneath the fan,
And the little
White man
All brown in shorts
Whisked me through
The swinging doors

And
There at last
You were,
"Good to see you
Let's go drink a beer."

1979

CLOWNS

Who is the clown?
"It is he," said she,
"For he cannot
Relate
Cannot sustain
The effort
To survive."

"He is not," said I,
"For I can see
He fumbles for
The truth
Of love and
Sin and hope
In Jesus."

"You are the clown,"
Said she,
"Who kneels upon
The ground and
Talks and stares
To empty air
Each morning of
The year."

1979

MAN MADE

These are what we made
In the moment of our lusting
Of our sweating and moaning
As we ripple in an echo
Of God's creating.

These are what we made
And why can they not speak
Or play or cry or sing
And why won't they die
We shout aloud
In God's bewailing.

These are what we made
And I cannot touch
And loath to see
The distorted image
Of you and me and
Cry out
In God's cursing.

These are what we cannot choose
To love
For they are us and
We are them and
We will stay and hold
And hold and
Share in God's salvation.

1979

19

TEARS

I am sorry
I can't comfort you
with words.

I am sorry
that you cannot
tell your pain.

All I can do
is hold you
close and warm.

And you in your
sweet innocence
please cry for me.

1979

BEING ONE OF THEM

We all stood
at our benches
scraping and
banging about.

In came some
visitors and
we all just
looked away.

"And what are
we making there
my dear?" one
said to me.

"A spice rack"
said I, "but
I am an ordinand
most of the time."

"Oh," said he and
gave me a knowing look,
"Keeps the old grey
matter busy, spice racks,
don't you think?"

"No, but I protest
I really am an ordinand
who comes to be
like one of them
one afternoon a week."

1979

21

OUR MAM

Our Mam,
Your sad eyes
Touch me
More
Than when they laughed
And danced
And sang.

Our Mam
When will you smile?
It does no good to cry.

Our Mam,
Somewhere
Darker
And more hidden
Than any womb
You struggle
To be born

And
I
Can't help you.

1980

TO SIÂN

Words are so
Silly
Don't you think?

It's daft to
Ask you
How it feels.

Silence
Grips us all
And all our
Fleeting touches
And eyes' caresses
Cannot express:

We're awkward
In the middle of all this.

Yet,
Somehow,
Quiet and unknown,
God laid his finger
On our youthful loins.

In secret
He has broken in
And given that
For which we
Dare not wish.

And so
In silence
We must wait
And see:

We three
Will grow
In mystery
Until we all
Are born.

And then
We have to
Speak aloud
And give
To it
A name.

1980

WEST MARSH GRIMSBY

From bleak salt marshes of
The Freshney dragged.
By timber from the mountains
Of the north
And flesh of fish from valleys
Of salt ice.

Lapped by Lincoln green and
Aired by brown-sea blows
That carry seagull's mournful wings
That wheel above
The grey smoke weeping
Chimney pots.

Tatty dogs patrol and shiny prams
Glide by
So far from Rasen's foothill feel and
So unlike
The earth of Cabourne's hill.

Fishmeal smell hangs round Cleveland Bridge
And soap flake
Lemon corner shops give way
A murky bare bulb
Light by day.

1981

GILBEY ROAD

The tide's gone out
On Gilbey Road;
Pigeons coo at the
Water's edge.

The washing line masts
Flap to mark
The covered wrecks.

Slow like shifting sand
They sit round-shouldered
At square gas fires,
Pumping back high
Water days of sail
And coal and tram cars
Humming down the road.

The tide's gone out
On Gilbey Road
And left brick flotsam
Where the marsh once spread;
And no one sees
New tides to cleanse
And wash away.

1981

BEN

Dear Ben
When you were small
I hardly dare touch you
At all.

It grows doesn't it?
Being a dad?
You really are my lad.

It's good to wrestle
In bed
It's good
To laugh with you:
You fill me up.

Even though you put
Your fingers in my ears.

1981

BRINGING IT ALL BACK HOME

Lots of things
Drag it back
Music and pictures
In the mind.

Memories are sensual:
I can taste
The breath
Often.

In the end
I cannot give them
To anyone.
I cannot preach
Memories.
Somehow our galleries
Must overlap.

That's why it's
Easier
To bring them all
Back home.

1982

HOARDINGS

Through the rain
Her breasts are bouncing bare,
Her lips are wet
Caressing her own hair.
She sucks in every
Passer by
And who can't say
She isn't pleasing
To a hungry eye.
But to say she touched
Our weakest spot
From a warehouse wall
By the commercial dock,
Just goes to show
How silly we all are.

1983

MY PEN

With this
Same pen
I have
Scratched
Around
In subjects
That confound
Me now.

I have
Prodded
The minds
Of Aberlard
And Beckett
And the like.

I have penned
The fall
Of many a king
And traced
Universal movements
Succinctly.

Since
Then
I line up
On the page
A talk of God.

I jumble
Schleiermacher and Barth
To fill
A space
Prompted
By our Lord.

After all this
What can
I say
Now
With this same pen?

I have to
Break an
Ordered thought
To peak at
Backsides
Of the truth.

I could say
Man is man
And
God is God
But.
That is obvious
To all
Especially those
Without a pen
Like mine.

1983

THE WIDOW AND THE PARROT

I tried to write about
The woman and the parrot:
I'd cracked many a smile
On that and wanted to
Get it down.

But it's so sad you have to
Laugh, really.
She had to sell it
Not because it talked like
Her old man,
And not because it attacked
Her through the bars,
But because she needed
Money;
To pay the Co-op funeral man.

1984

GOD OF SURPRISES

Picture God.
Surely you can?
Can't you fit Him in your camera?
Can't you sing Him in your song?
Surely you can? You Can!

Picture God.
If you dare!
Can't you draw a picture of everything?
Can't you sing in all keys at once?
Surely you can? Can't you?

Picture God.
If you can!
Can't you remember a surprise?
Can't you feel joy, shock, love?
Surely you can? You can!

1985

OFFERTORY HYMN

What shall we lay on your table good Lord?
What shall we bring to this feast of your love?
What shall we offer, standing before you?
Ready and listening – what do you ask?

> *Place on my table the plate of your hoping,*
> *Place on my table the cup of your dreams,*
> *Offer to me all your deepest desiring*
> *And I will provide all the food for the feast.*

Bring me in trust all hearts that are broken;
Bent down by pain and ground down by life's
    grief.
Bring me the fruits of your labour in loving;
Bring me them sour and bring me them sweet.

> *Place on my table the plate of your hoping,*
> *Place on my table the cup of your dreams,*
> *Offer to me all your deepest desiring*
> *And I will provide all the food for the feast.*

Bring me the water from joy's overflowing,
Bring me the tears that have never been shed.
Bring me the love that lives in each family,
Bring me youth's dreams and all that age
    dreads.

> *Place on my table the plate of your hoping,*
> *Place on my table the cup of your dreams,*
> *Offer to me all your deepest desiring*
> *And I will provide all the food for the feast.*

These are the tears I shed in the garden,
This is the love of the Galilee shore,
Yours is the joy that I knew in my own home,
Yours are the fears of that Friday at noon.

Place on my table the plate of your hoping,
Place on my table the cup of your dreams,
Offer to me all your deepest desiring
And I will provide all the food for the feast.

All of your life is made rich by my living,
All of your dying made hope by my death;
I will give you the love of forgiveness,
Share all the gifts of God's tenderness.

Place on my table the plate of your hoping,
Place on my table the cup of your dreams,
Offer to me all your deepest desiring
And I will provide all the food for the feast.

1986

CONKERS

I have looked high
In a conker tree,
And I have seen
The biggest conkers
You ever could see.

Ben and Davy
How I would love to
Bring them down,
They would be fun
And the best around.

Hannah and Little Liz
How I would love to
Fill your tiny hands
With their warm smooth brown.

But I am so sad,
I cannot climb
that high,
I cannot throw a stick
That far.
But,
I have a friend
And he has told me something.

He has told me
He will send the wind,
And in the morning
They will be down
Among the leaves;
And there
Even the little ones
Will fill
Their pockets with them.

We will go
Together.
Every day,
And look.
Cross
My heart.

1987

THE WEDDING AT CANA

I.   THE THIRD DAY

In the echoing harmony
of the third day,
in the virgin moment
of a new world;
the waters of creation break,
yielding from the deep
the fruitful ground;
growing from the goodness of God.

In the dancing rhythms
of the third day,
in the innocent ecstasy
of celebration
heaven's son takes flesh
in passionate embrace,
making joy
from a new world's wine.

In the silent dawning
of the third day,
in the new expecting light,
the garden murmurs
its mystery; -
the retreating tide
of the water
of death.

1988

II. THE WATERS OF LOVE

The water of love flows
from God's heart;
like rain, like a river
to quench the parched.
The strength of the tide,
the still ocean deeps
the pounding on conscience
the caressing of dreams.

The water of love wells
from man's heart;
sweet tears of love's pain
and hard tears of regret.
The springs of forgiveness,
the deep pool of peace
are found in each person
and yearn for release.

The waters of love,
human and divine,
when mingled create
the most beautiful wine.
In the glass of life's living
in the joy of our hearts
the waters are joined
and will never part.

1988

III. THE SERVANTS' SONG

It is the empty-handed
that grasp the richness of God.

Only the broken-hearted
hear the healing words
of unbroken silence.

Only in those whose lives are spent
the fruit of love is grown.

It is the eyes that watch the world
that see the mystery unfold.

For only a servant can know in truth
the will of the slave to all.

To a servant
the gift is
a wounded heart
a cup of bitter wine,
which poured through
tender blood-red hands
all creation binds.

1988

MILKING TIME

We watched the cows
Go by,
Sixty-six of them –
Two little girls and I.

I knelt on one knee
And held them
One in each arm
As the swaying beasts
Passed by.

They were in no hurry
But knew where to go;
No one to lead;
An old man followed with
His dog.

They were shiny in the sun
The noses wet and drippy,
Their large eyes
Reflecting
The two little girls and I.

1988

DIVINE LOVERS

One day
We will be
Divine
Lovers.
Embracing
Naked heart
To
Naked heart.
Penetrating
Utterly;
Knowing
Stainless
Ecstasy.

1990

CONSOLATION

God is creator of dark and light;
And he speaks in both.
Both teem and crawl with creation.
It is in the night
That the ear is tuned
To that whispered voice,
That seldom speaks in the course of day.

To this voice
We must bend our being;
Touch the crown and
Smell the blood.
In the dark
The inner eye can bear the light
Which is the lamb.

And the tears that are shed
In the meeting
Are not the tears of sorrow;
They are not pain:
They are a sacrament
Of being fully alive.

1990

What we
Think is not
What is spoken.
What is spoken
Is seldom
Heard.
What is seldom
Heard
Is rarely
Said.

The mind cannot
Wrap its
Clumsy hand
Around it
But lets it fall
Breaking;
Picking it up
In unrecognisable pieces
That only bread can hold.

1990

THE WOMAN AT THE ALTAR

Beyond the monstrance
I saw
A beautiful girl
In chasuble clothed;
Her hair cascading
Down the glittering gold.

She lifted high
Above her
The Host;
Disclosing
Her bursting belly,
Beating with child.

She cracked the Bread's back
With gentle hands,
And I heard
The searing scream
Of her unborn child.

There was no chalice.
The blood
Is in the paschal rhythm,
Is in the waxing and waning,
Is in the hidden womb
Where only God
Can walk.

And I,
Only a priest,
So easily spent and afraid,
Wept to ease
My aching mind.

1990

THE FAR SEEING LAND

I. CHAPEL ST. LEONARDS

The little boy stands on his castle of sand,
and gazes across the far seeing land.
The marram grass armies below him snake,
and crashing behind, brown sea horses break.

He looks and he sees beyond and beyond,
the marsh and the meadow, his house and
beyond
the red-roofed church, the scots-pine-hid farm,
beyond where the London train whistle alarms.

Further, higher, than a fairy tale cloud
he sees beyond villages, woods and the towns -
where the lessening spires meet the wide wold
green,
and earth touches sky in a place unseen.

Above him, around him, he's crowned with the
sky,
and over his shoulders the grey clouds fly;
with his heart in the stars and his feet in the
sand,
forever a king of the far-seeing land.

1990

II. MARKET RASEN and WILLINGHAM WOODS

Willingham's sand breaks the wide wolds'
wave.
Where the forest greens blue on Hamilton Hill.
Drenched in scents of fresh cut pine,
he seeks her heart in cow brown eyes.
His whole being yearns an answer in dreams;
a thousand tomorrows in places unseen.

Five winters go. Six summers come.
Cobblestoned Saturday market hums.
The sand stone porch frames man and wife,
Crowned King and Queen of each others' life.
An end, a beginning, another beyond;
wild bells echo the far-seeing land.

1990

III. LINCOLN CATHEDRAL

In
the swan man's
soaring song of
stone, the twin
tower exultet of
wold and fen.
Whose rose eye
searches far and near
colouring sunrises
of everymans' year.
Under vaulted sky
which eternity spans
spangled with sound
only heaven can own.

Here
a man kneels to
take in his hands
the fisherman's keys
of the kingdom
that stands every tide.
With his heart in the
stars and his feet
in the sand he is
ordained a dreamer,
a gazer, a bringer to
light, of treasure
hidden beyond each
every days' sight.

1990

IV. WEST MARSH, GRIMSBY

The tide had turned on Gilbey Road.
The swing bridge stuck,
split the silent dock.
Terraced wave upon wave
break upon the blue buses
ploughing streets beyond
Humbers' strand.
Pyewipe's smoke and
Laporte's cloud scent the
fluorescent rain falling
from the starless dark.

Now a father of double kind;
with little boys, new worlds to see.
Schooled in love by The King of Love;
his heart is woven through
a thousand thresholds.
A bearer of words
to silent firesides,
seeing beyond back doors
the house with many rooms.

Dreaming other dreams,
fearing the fright of those
whose life is sand.
Knowing the crown of love
has many piercing points;
a compass of light
in the farseeing
daylight dark.   *1990*

V. LUTTON MARSH

Stammering sparrows cannot stir
the sleeping house.
Little ones dream still, safe in the
warming dawn.
He stands alone at the window and gazes
beyond at
strawberry pullers bent tall on the
far-seeing land,
the sun stealing the ripeness from
under their hands.
Beyond, the dyke squared
table cloth spreads the
ripening corn and flowering rape
out to Guy's Head,
where the lighthouses wag fingers
at the Nene's brown tide.

His heart is caught again with
the strongest pulse;
the silent still rhythm in sun, sea and soil,
in the sweet smell of earth drenched
in glittering dew,
In the sunlight crowning his
sleeping wife's hair.
In the gift of each morning's
Te Deum his whole being sings,
Thou art God and we praise you! Amen.

1990

VI. GEDNEY DAWSMERE CHURCHYARD

Where earth and sky mingle
in the cup of The Wash;
where the curlew's cry
fills the empty sky.

Neath the pall of cloud
on an August day;
the priest and the people
wait by a grave.

The low brick church
tolls its one dull bell;
the coffin rests gently
in earth's cockleshells.

The age of the man
who lies in the grave,
is the same as the man
who stands up and prays.

One man was drowned
in a fenland drain;
one seeks to lose
what other man save.

The priest at the parting
lifts high his hand,
and blesses by shadow
the far-seeing land.

1990

I WILL MAKE YOU FISHERS OF MEN

I.   THE FLY FISHERMAN

A stalking man
With delicate rod and
Feathery flies that
Hiss off fluent
Lengths of line at
A practised flick.

A sporting man
That operates
Intelligently
By deceit,
To play the game
In places where only
Landrovers can climb.

1991

II. THE COARSE FISHERMAN

A waiting man
Whose patience is a sitting
One, a watching one,
That knows they
Will bite.
But if they
Don't the fresh air's
Good and bright.

A silent man
Who punctuates the river
With a match or two
And if, by luck, he
Catches some he'll
Let them swim away
For him to fool another day.

1991

III. THE DRAG NET

A hopeful man
Whose net is stretched
Between the tattered
Breakwaters to catch
The shoals that may
Come with the sea.

A faithful man
Returning after every tide
In dark or light,
To pick the sea weed
From the wave-wrung net,
And set the line 'till
It is taut again.

1991

IV. THE DEEPSEA FISHERMAN

A gambling man
Who turns his back
On sport and cuts the
Land lines clean to
Take to white and grey
To keep those few old wolves away.

A fearless man
That casts his nets
So deep and tries his
Arm to wrestle with
The wind.
And all
To feed fish fingers
To the rest.

1991

THE SONG OF GUTHLAC[1]

By the twisted black waters of
this desert-fen, a man of God came.
On Crow land his hermit hut made
where the grave-robbed barrow lay.
In this landscape of lostness he
journeyed to find the pearl of great price;
The Way, Truth, Life of all mankind.

A warrior by birth; "Guthlac" his name,
"The fruit of war" in the English tongue,
"Bella Munis" in Latin's more elegant frame.
With the torrents of youth had Guthlac swam;
by sword and spear fame his right hand had
        gained.
'Till one deep night, in still dreams of dark,
his hungry heart woke to the waste of his days.

In the merciful light of the sun's morning rays
the enemies of Christ he promised to slay;
courage, mind, spirit and strength sacrificed
to the service of God to the close of his life.
At Repton the three-fold vows he made;
the armour of Jesus on his body he laid;
faith's shield, hope's helmet, the word's double
        blade.

---

[1] For Lincoln Male Voice Choir

57

This warrior still hungered the fiercest fight;
The endless wrestle of the hermit's life.
With prayers and blessings to the fen he came
the battle to join in the Devil's domain.
On Bartholomew's Day did the Holy Man land,
and in the saint's company took his stand
to vanquish the demons who reigned the
     Crowland.

1992

STRONG TOWER[2]

I.   CHRISTMAS NIGHT

Only
just
in this world.
Moonlit rooftops
touch
the wheeling stars.

The strong tower
catches
and returns
the light.

Above all
the resurrection
colours fly.
The red cross
shimmers
in the silver sky.

1992

---

[2] For Martin Pickering

59

II. RINGERS' REQUIEM

How the bells ring
in the January night!
Shaking the stars.
Rising.
Falling.

In your coffin
still
the changes ring;
your body baptized
in the deep
waves of sound.

1992

III. CEDAR OF LEBANON

Decades
have drifted down the centuries
as you have thrown wide your arms:

Exultant
with the bride.
Everlasting arms
over the
mourner's head.
Yet you exist for these moments –
the winter's evenings,
when your hidden boughs
throw down
the dying light
on the shade-bound
graves.

1992

IV. ST MICHAEL & ALL ANGELS EDENHAM

I come to lose myself in you,
you ancient walls, you well-worn pews;
your lime-washed walls echo my prayer
and your still still silence comforts care.

Known to all and yet my secret place,
by your first light I seek His face;
I come alone and yet find company:
faithful souls who worshipped here before me.

You are my treasury of the old and new,
you show me the Ancient and Renewing Truth;
the beauty that you hold within this space
was made by man on fire with Heavenly
Grace.

My every sense in you is made alive:
you touch my ears, my nose, you fill my eyes;
in you, stone and light, bright colours and dark
wood
proclaim the language of the flesh made word.

You are my touching and my meeting place;
in death, in birth, in love and in disgrace
I find myself face down upon your floor
to plead, to thank, to worship and adore.

By All Angels and their captain you are named.
Your bells, your strong white tower, Gospel
Truth proclaim;
you stood tall when this village was yet young.
To you in ancient tongues His praise was sung.

You are to me a comfort and a gracious gift.
I see you and from this mean world my mind
lifts;
You teach me and the graves around your walls
To look to things that last – the end of all.

I come to lose myself in you,
You ancient walls, you well-worn pew;
By letting go I hope to find
The Way, Truth, Life of all mankind.

1992

RAPE

Penetrating
My eyes
Shocking
Unearthly yellow.

Its stench
Robbing
The sweet May day
Of air.

I detest
The weeping eyes.
Its long strong
Lingering
Presence.

1992

DEEP HARVESTS[3]

Living silver lies
in ever-climbing valleys of salt-ice.
Deep.
Hid.
Dark.
In silent stillness,
it seams, glides, moves,
below the brown buffet,
the shock, spray, spume.

Miners search
the unseen shimmer.
Men apart,
befriending death
in wind and wave.

In breaking days,
empty,
quiet,
they draw near,
drenched by disappointment
of the strain and strain
by light and night.

Yet from East's horizon
they can rise
and greet St Mary's light
with rough-voiced cry,

---

[3] For South Shields Choral Society

their decks with silver
stacked up high.

And as they land
beneath
where moon tides
never turn,
beneath
the silent shoals,
a metal net is shot,
heavy with men plummeting
to the silver black.

Beneath
the heaving sea
a harvest is hewn
in close-aired dangers
by submariners in rock,
whose strain and strain
in endless night
keep home fires warm.

Till drawn up
from the dark,
drinking the hard sea air,
they greet the evening light
like early dawn.

1993

BROKEN BODY

There is a pain that is
Both mine and yours.
I did not make it
And yet I am its cause.

Once we were one body
And now we are de-formed.
We ate one bread and
Now we starve alone.

The common tongue we used
Is now for each confused.
We speak the word
Yet hear no sense at all.

A past we shared
Today's hurt takes its toll.
I fear the future,
Parting is all it holds.

1993

MYSTICAL UNION

Marriage.

My hand
On your side.

My palm
Cupped in your waist.

Is held
In wonder.

By
A slender
Silk-silver
Crescent moon.

By
A sun-white
Wave-washed
Bay.

Ripples
Play
At my touch:
Scattering
Light.

1993

EASTER MEN

Widowed men
Both
With their broken
Families
Listening;
Stand up
Giving
The Word
Voice.

Tenderly
Chiding
The neighbours
Who are embarrassed
By death,
(If they were here
To hear).

These men
In darkest winter
Were Easter Men;
Bending their being
To The Truth.

Deaf
To the hammer blows
That shout –
"The dark
Fixed Him
In stone."

He is Life.
They give Him
Voice by being.
Their daily works
Are
Easter bells
And Alleluias.

1993

NUNS AND FLAMINGOS

Over the convent wall
The flamingo pool stands.
Its tall pink occupants
Bow and bow again.

On the other side
The sisters dressed in black
Dip their hearts
Into the deep.

1993

MORNING PRAYER

Sound settles in
The quiet church.
Lorry's brake.
Playground scream.
The lost lamb.
Lofty church-tower pigeon call.

The morning sun
Breaks the eastern glass;
The paschal candle's
Fresh flame
Dances.

The first words
Bids God to
Make us speak.
With unseen hosts
We worship
And bow down.

These prayers
Are not ours.
We are the new voice
In an ancient place.

The last AMEN
Is one
With all
Who went before;
With lamb and lorry,
And the childrens' call.   *1994*

THE STABLE CHAPEL

Jacob took a
Stone,
One shaped like
A pillow and dreamt.
Here a ladder
Had grown
Dream-like.
To become a gate of heaven.
We took this
Old stable
Long vacant of horses;
With its falling ceiling;
Its cobbled floor;
Its doubled door
And chimney.
Long before
Anyone said a prayer,
Or lifted The Host,
We dreamed
What it
Now
Is.

1994

TEXT FOR TALLIS' CANON

Moments of meeting, rare and true;
reveal a beauty hid from view:
the harmony of heaven that sounds
where symmetry in life is found.

The sweetness of a lover's kiss,
the tenderness of a caress,
can plunge the depths of empty hearts
and heralds tears when friendship parts.

No human mind, nor earth bound scheme
can recreate these undreamt dreams;
when for a moment space and time
created order sounds with rhyme.

A bird's reflection in a lake
the scent of hay in summer heat,
the sounds of bells on Christmas night,
the comfort of a home's fire light.

These precious gifts are love revealed;
moment by moment they are weaved
into the pattern of our lives
to hold, to cherish, then take flight.

1994

THE LAND

I. WINTER

Wildfowl
like snow
lie thick on Drove End Marsh.
The leaden
fill-dyke sky
makes Gedney's church tower
bright.

There is no winter
here,
though peat-black soil
and silt still sleep.
In villages of glass
the sun caresses
growth of green
on slender goose-necked
daffodils.

There is no winter
here,
though empty, silent days
pass by.
Each hand,
Each eye,
Each mind,
Each heart
yearns
for the ever-dawning
light.

There is no winter
here
but only growing.
This land defies
the dark.
Three seasons only:
every day
a harvest.

1995

II. SPRING

*As I woke one May morning, one May morning
so early,
I overtook a pretty fair maid just as the sun was
dawning.
With my rue rum ray, fother diddle ay, wok fol
air did-dle ido!*

Sharp spinning steel renews the ground.
The harrow runs to the seagulls' sound.
The dark clouds part for the waxing sun.
The land is alive – a new season's begun.

In soft deep silt, fresh patterns weave
the ridge and furrow of potato fields.
Winter wheat deepens to rich shining greens
and moves to the touch of a warming breeze.

The spring showers wash the brightening sky.
Vans and lorries on muddy lanes fly.
The skyline is dinted by machines and men;
their lights crawl late on marsh and fen.

These are the days when the best work is done,
When land is fit and machine's on song.
These are the hours that must not be missed;
when the earth and the weather for a brief
moment kiss.

When the gates are shut and the tools washed down,
there is a silent growing in the dark moist ground,
till hour by hour in the fields spreads a blaze,
with the crackling of colour that is louder each day.

See rich gold of daffodils by Moulton's tall spire!
See pink of the pipe flowers where marshes spread far!
See rainbow of colours where bulb fields burst!
See brightest of rape from the blackest of earth!

When Holbeach and Whaplode towers Easter peels ring,
The land with its own resurrection hymn sings!
Through fields and through church yards, from altar to pew,
teems a torrent of colour the whole county
through!

1995

III. SUMMER

There is beauty in each season,
There is beauty in each sky,
There is beauty as the land unfolds
all colours to the eye.

In winter there is waiting.
In spring there is new hope.
And autumn sings thanksgiving
for all that summer's wrought.
Yet only in the summer
the sky lark rises high,
and fills the fields with song
from a brilliant, cloudless sky.

Long lanes stretch far-shimmering –
By the dry brown dykes;
poplar avenues stand crowned
by crystal clear sunlight.
There is a gentle murmuring
Among the fruiting gangs.
Where they stack the trays for market,
A rich, sweet fragrance hangs.

The corn is white perfection
and ripples like the sea;
through it ploughs the combine
showering plumes of dust like spray.
The blades beat out a rhythm,
the well-tuned engine hums;
man, land machine in harmony,
a new harvest has begun.

Through villages and hamlets
the corn carts rumble by;
the procession keeps on moving –
while the night sky is dry.
And in the sheds the driers
give out a mighty roar
as the mountains of pure gold
climb higher from the floor.

There is a summer landscape
where a tractor's seldom seen,
where the air is stung with salt
and silt mingles with the sea.
Here the samphire yields its harvest,
and the mullet swims each tide,
and villages of seals meet
on sun-warmed sand to dry.

1995

IV. AUTUMN[4]

When I was bound apprentice in famous
Lincolnshire,
Full well I served my master for more than
seven year,
Till I took up to poaching, as you will quickly
hear;
Oh, 'tis my delight on a shining night, in the
season of the year!

Delight! Delight!
The land delights!
Sky is bright
with harvest moon.

Delight! Delight!
The land delights!
Joyful shouts bring
harvest home.

Delight! Delight!
Each farm delights!
Orchard boughs
hang heavy now.

Delight! Delight!
Each farm delights!
Land turns dark
behind the plough.

---

[4] Incorporating the traditional English folksong,
The Lincolnshire Poacher

Delight! Delight!
Machines delight!
Empty earth eats
this year's seed.

Delight! Delight!
Machines delight!
Turning steel meets
hunger's need.

*As me an' my companion were setting off a
snare,*
*'Twas then we spied the game keeper, for him
we did not care,*
*For we can wrestle and fight, my boys, and
jump out anywhere,*
*Oh, 'tis my delight on a shining night, in the
season of the year!*

*As me an' my companion were setting four or
five,*
*And, taking on 'en up again, we caught a hare
alive,*
*We took the hare alive, my boys, and through
the woods did steer;*
*Oh, 'tis my delight on a shining night, in the
season of the year!*

Delight! Delight!
Daylight delights!
Church fills up
with apples' smell.

Delight! Delight!
Daylight delights!
Harvest hymns
God's goodness tell.

Delight! Delight!
The moon delights!
Settling earth
its rest begins.

Delight! Delight!
The moon delights!
Fields grow quiet
as night draws in.

*I threw him on my shoulder and we trudged
home,
We took him to a neighbour's house and sold
him for a crown,
We sold him for a crown, my boys, but I did
not tell you where;
Oh, 'tis my delight on a shining night, in the
season of the year!*

Delight! Delight!
Our hearts delight!
Dance sounds rise
from village hall.

Delight! Delight!
Our hearts delight!
Priest says grace
for groaning board.

Success to every gentleman who lives in
Lincolnshire,
Success to every poacher who wants to sell a
hare,
Bad luck to every game keeper that will not sell
his deer;
Oh, 'tis my delight on a shining night, in the
season of the year!

Delight! Delight!
The land delights!
All is safely
gathered in.

Delight! Delight!
The land delights!
The earth is in its
fullness crowned.

1995

WAITING FOR THE LORD

Waiting is
The harmony of hope
Drawn
From faith's strumming
At our need.

Waiting is
The open hand
Of trusting
In a parent
By a child.

Waiting is
The singing silence
Of the heart
In tune with
The Advent Key.

1995

THE LAMB'S LIGHT

By The Lamb's
light walk.
Of His Easter
morn talk.
Death's dark
cannot
reveal the way
that ends in
everlasting day.

1995

THE FERRY

Under Easter's
Sharp-showering sky.
Walking among
Wind-driven shadows,
I came to the
Wide river.

Faithfully,
I followed the signs –
"To the ferry".

In a boat house
I found
The ferry man;
The fragrance of
Paint and pine
Filled the low room.

He knelt before
A new boat
Gently polishing.
It was beautiful.

Its wood
In gentle rhythms
Moved and met,
Meeting in
A brass-capped bow.
Copper nails
Glistened
In the dark hull.

"Have I found the ferry?"
I enquired.
He beckoned me.
"It is finished.
I make three a year
Christmas, Easter, Michaelmas".

"Help me to Christen her".
Together we pulled.
She stood silent,
In the deep water.

Obediently.
Silently.
I stepped in.
Suddenly
We were in the light.
The bow
Breaking the waters.
By long moments
Of satisfaction
He brought me to
The distant shore.

"The journey is free,"
He said,
"Be careful on your way."

1996

OLD LADIES

The strongest people
Are held up
By frames.
They live on
Memory and duty.
Femininity
Is not dimmed
By age.
Their loveliness
Is not in beauty.

1997

TWO LOVES

I love two loves –
one of them is sweet
one of the them is sweeter than
an angel's touch or taste.

In the you I love
is the thou I seek;
heaven's mystery is hid
in your eye-deeps.

Your voice, your breath
gives silent love song;
to you the ear of my being
listens and longs.

Hold me, bury me
in your tender embrace;
in the ever-dawning light
my soul shall awake.

1997

WHO CAN DENY?

I would that
my life
were a beautiful thing:
A thank you in all
for everything.

You have
out of nothing
made all that is;
your life
you give
that I may live.

I see
my children
in their sleep,
I watch
my love
our home-life keep;

I hear
my brother
at his work.
I love them
with a strength
that hurts.

Look up
in awe
at starred nightscapes;
look out
and taste
as brown waves break.

Who can deny
that joy,
that truth,
that crowds upon us
on the way?

Who can resist
the yearning deep
that moves out heart,
its meaning seek?

O come!
Let us
echo the call
that fashions
and sustains us all.

1998

COMPOSTELLA

The 'field of stars' - is not a place.
It is not just a dream.
'Field of Stars' is when the heart
Is filled, toiled and rent and
Yields a treasure dearly spent.

The 'field of stars' - is not a place.
It is not just a dream.
Its treasure is the birth-stone star
That wise men yearn for from afar;
Who by life's pilgrimages find
The new born who is Lord of Time.

The 'field of stars' - is not a place.
It is not just a dream.
It is the new born at the breast
Of she, 'above all women blessed'
Whose human flesh and blood could hold
The one who made the stars unfold.

The 'field of stars' - is not a place.
It is not just a dream.
'Field of stars' is when a
Fisherman's bones are dressed in gold:
Zebedee's Son who drained the cup of
A bitter draught his Lord had supped.

The 'field of stars' - is not a place.
It is not just a dream.
'Field of stars' is when
You and I in truth can say –
"Yes!" Your will be done in me
And body, mind and soul agree.

2000

THE COUNTRY PARSON'S PILGRIMAGE

By the waters at Blaye we laid down and slept;
A Napoleonic fortress our bicycles kept.
We said Evensong – as in 'Common Prayer';
Then John washed his socks and I washed my
    hair!

Across foreign rivers our pilgrimage passed
By the Charente's green flow, the Ardour's
    deep gash;
But here at Blaye, a small ferry boot plied
The treacherous mouth of Gironde's' tide.

Before us there stretched the Landes' tall trees,
And lush green meadows of the Pyrenees;
The heat of the sun on Meseta's plain,
The full-bodied, chilled, red wine of Spain.

We prayed Morning Prayer in village churches.
We sang our hymns and Coverdale's verses.
We read our way through the Book of Acts –
And heard how St James lost his head, by an
    axe.

So we passed, two English parsons
By El Cid's statue and baroque fountains
And came at last to St James' shrine –
- Apostle dressed up Spanish style.

Were we less English for our journey?
Did we return more tanned and friendly?
Did we come home and after meals
Prefer cafe con leche instead of tea?

There was a change, I have no doubt;
It will take much prayer to work it out;
But we were certain by journey's end
That God is not an Anglican!

2000

WATERFALL

The lake lies still
Within the folded hills:
Myriad streams in
Ceaseless movement
Empty into one silence.

Where – beyond sight –
The valley opens up its arms
There is release:
     The ecstasy of
        Breaking,
           Falling,
              Tumbling
                  On the shining rock.
The power
Shuddering and shaking
The mist-hung air.

2000

QUANTA QUALIA

O anima mea
Mane!
O quanta qualia
Conventus gaudia
Erunt.

O my soul
Wait!
O how great and how wonderful
the joys of meeting
will be.

2002

EDENHAM 1988 – 2003[5]

Economia.
So the Fathers
Described the cost
And benefits
Of God's mercy:
Spent on His beloved creation:
Spent in His enfleshing
Of Eternal Truth:
Spent for the broken-hearted
Prisoner of darkness
On a Friday
In His own
Blood.

Economia
Is a mystery:
It is beyond
Binary calculation;
It is beyond
Theological
Definition.
Love:
loving and self-giving.
Love
Can darkly
Grasp its truth.

---

[5] On the decision of Lincoln Diocese to withdraw
financial support

Economia
Is partaking
In the gracious gift –
The fullness of Glory
The right way:
God
Given.

We together
Have spent ourselves
In this old house
With its half-hidden well
And Cedars of Lebanon.
Within Economia
Our children
Have grown.

Now.
In this present time;
As you take this in:
Economy confronts Economia
World against Word.
It is the adversary
Crude
Materialism;
Whose ideology
Is merciless
Equality.

Such cruel certainties
Profit
By spiritual death
And bankruptcy.

In your charity
Pray for us
Jesus mercy!

2003

DRESSED IN BLUE

In heavenly
blue
of stained-glass
you are
dressed.
Within
your heart
a raging sea
could rest.

Distant stars
are woven
in your hair.
Your sweet
and gentle
touch
can heal
all care.

You are
Mother,
Lover,
Bride
and Friend.
Your life of
simple service
has no end.

Your love
and beauty
will not,
cannot,
die.
You are
creation
in perfection:
the apple
of His eye.

2003

BLUE IN BLUE

Horizon:
Sky
In
Sea;
Meeting;
Parting;
Mystery.

2003

TRES AMORES

Caritas –
One love;
is strength
to give.

Delecta –
Two loves;
to sing
the heart's
delight.

Concordia –
Three loves
to bind
the world
as one.

Tres Amores.

2003

MYSTERIUM

Mysterium in amicitia est
Mysterium in vita est.

Solutio inventerest in amore;
Solutio inventerest in veritate.

There is mystery in friendship
There is mystery in life.

The solution is found in love;
The solution is found in truth.

2003

REFLEXIONEM

Veritas vertuatem redit.
Pulchritudo veritatem redit.

Truth reflects goodness.
Beauty reflects truth.

2004

A SONNET OF THANKYOUS

One half one hundred is a decent score,
And is, for certain, cause to pop a cork
Or two – and then to contemplate some more!
With friends, of course, to provide support.
So it was one week short of Christmas Day,
I was surprised by loved ones near and far
A wintry afternoon we lunched and sang away
And many gifts they carried from their cars!
There were yet more surprises still to come
Next day, when Sunday service had been
    prayed
My flock assembled and Happy Birthday sung -
Yet more gifts their care and love displayed.
There are few times in life so sweet and good.
For you I daily thank my loving God.

2004

JESUS WEPT

Eyes, come and see the hard cold stone of
    death.
See, and then know, the loss and fear in grief.
Know, and then fear, the pain within His will;
and see prefigured there Golgotha's hill.

Eyes, run with tears that spring from pity's care;
pity that flows from Love's desire to share.
Love pity me who Death for love will bear.
Weep and still weep: death's sure decay is
    near.

I lift up my eyes and beyond sense and sound
I see the mystery of Glorious love unbound;
love not bound by reason, time or death:
the gift of hope; the warm touch of His breath.

2005

THE VAUDAY PART SONGS

I.   THE OAKS

The landscape honours you;
Ancient and last-living.
Your sap's tide recedes far
Beyond history's telling.
Being still, rooted by the way,
You mock our passing present.
Listening to the language of your leaves,
We hear the sounds before music:
Ancestral voices speaking truths
In tongues we cannot understand.

2005

II. STONE

You lay for ages hidden under ground,
Shapeless, you waited, dark and dressed in dirt.
Then for a Holy purpose you were found
And hewn, cut, measured; dressed for mason's
    work.
For Abbey walls and towers you were made
To form a sacred space for heavenly sound.
Made cruciform and risen by their blades
That monks, their lives on living rock, might
    found.
Three centuries pass, the fire of worship dies;
No more you echo as the brothers sing.
Reformers' hammers smash and break your
    choir
To be rebuilt as lodging for a king.
Now for a noble use you lovely stand;
A nobler purpose quarried you from land.

2005

III. THE CARRIAGEWAY

Horse chestnut candles light the carriageway
Which from the highest point the park surveys
The distant house that dips behind the trees,
Then sweeps through open farmland green
    with wheat.

The wooden bridge with white rails Vauday
    keeps
Separate, secret, where ancient memory sleeps.
The steep wooded valley nave-like arches high;
In dappled green cool shade the cattle lie.

Then out into the open park it runs
Past shining water drowned in morning sun,
And, high above, the house all stately stands
And crowns the oak-dressed pasture land.

The journey made through park and wooded
    grange
Pass by a thousand years of chance and
    change.
The carriageway in classic splendour ends,
Proving the certain permanence of men.

2005

IV. IN MEMORIAM

Here
sorrow seeks solace
and tender memories refine;
light falls in from windows
set on high;
windows that deny
the outside eye.

Here
in this house
of many rooms
is one of still simplicity;
a place where
the yolk of life's complexity
is set upon His shoulder.

Here
when doors are closed
the sweetest
deepest silence
is received;
that echoes
with the Word
begotten
before time.

2005

THE FEAST

A festive table feeds
Both heart and eye.
For there is seen displayed
The fruit of earth and sky.
The universe is held
Within a table framed;
Food gives voice to truths
Too vast for simple names.
Bread, wine and water.
Honey, milk and lamb;
Are the meeting place
Of God and man.

2006

THE PRODIGAL'S SONG

I had a mind to make my way,
to see the world, to have my say.
My Father granted my request
and gave me early his bequest.

Soon into a wicked crowd I fell,
in everything bad my mind would dwell;
all the good things my Father gave
could not from death my spirit save.

All that was so freely given
I spent in vain – to make earth heaven,
until friendless, penniless, myself did sell
and find myself in living hell.

And there amid the swine and swill
I came to hate my selfish will
and thought upon my Father's farm
where my family lived all safe from harm.

And so myself I found at last
and humbly went to mend the past
and found my Father waiting there,
my every need His only care.

Not in the wealth of gold and jewels
my Father's endless love is found,
but in His forgiving tender arms –
here I rest. I am safe and sound.   *2006*

GOD OF EARTH AND HEAVEN

God of earth and heaven,
you made all from nothing.
You have made us, for yourself,
to reveal your likeness.
Open our eyes Lord
to see your will;
strengthen our hearts Lord
to love and worship you.

God of truth and beauty
holy and all mighty,
you have called us, one by one,
to become your children.
Open our lives Lord
to all your gifts.
Strengthen our hearts Lord
to love and worship you.

God of hope and healing
source of light and goodness,
we are yearning and we thirst
for the living water.
Open our minds Lord
to know your truth;
strengthen our hearts Lord
to love and worship you.

God of flesh and spirit
born of a Blessed Mary;
you have taught us
the law of love:
Open our lips Lord
to sing your praise
strengthen our hearts Lord
to love and follow you.

Jesus friend and brother
you reveal our Father.
Bless the poor and
heal the sick,
forgive the sinner.
Open our arms Lord
to embrace you.
Strengthen our lives Lord
to love and live in you.

2006

HEARTS OF ENGLAND

By the sea's rolling tide;
By the wide pennine sky;
By the skill found in
shipyard and mine;
By raw courage and love
when the journey is rough,
the hearts of England are made.

By bonds thicker than blood,
binding evil with good;
By the strength both of
family and home;
In the furnace of hope
on the anvil of will
the hearts of England are made.

Stand up men of steel
and let all the world feel
the skill of your hand
and your eye:
By sweet victory in game,
by faith and through pain
the hearts of England are made.

2008

LINCOLN CATHEDRAL (2)

This space:
A foretaste of heaven;
Spangled with sound.
Is built on bones.

So many
For so long
Have sought to have a place here.
Now
Marked by brass or stone
They sought permanence
In this house of God.

Walked over
And ignored;
They are a curiosity.
Some are faintly ridiculous:
Old honours unregarded;
Decades of service
Mocked by centuries.

The building itself
Has a ridiculous quality;
A stone skeleton:
It's only flesh
The thin skin
Of bread
Lifted high
In the side chapel,
Built for yet
more bones.   *2009*

TRANSFIGURATION

Uncreated inner light
Breaking out
In lighting white.
Brilliance beyond compare;
Two men of fire
In prayer partaking;
Prefiguring you and I:
Our baptismal flame
Still burning;
Our hearts to Him
In turning;
The darkening glass
Removing;
His glory to us
Transfiguring
To us His glory.

2009

CURE OF SOULS

I cannot sanctify
Your table.
The cyclical hospitality
Of prosperity
Sickens me.
I make you awkward
When I mention
Grace.
Yet
I am bound to you;
I made vows
Sealed with blood
That is not mine.

2009

SWINSTEAD SUMMER SUNDAY

Timeless quiet
Rests
On every home;
The churchyard, lawn-like,
Shines
With dew.
In little St Mary's
The door is open wide,
The bright air fresh with
Bird-song
Colours the silence inside.
The altar dressed for offering
Is transfigured in sunlight.
Beyond the clear east window
Horse-chestnuts lift up high.
Such beauty beyond refining:
The gentlest touch of love's desiring.

2010

EYE TO EYE

In embracing
lovers return
tenderness
by gazing
eye to eye.

In meeting
friends renew
their trust
by gazing
eye to eye.

In caring
mothers guide
their child
by speaking
eye to eye.

Peace-making
between us
will begin
by looking
eye to eye.

2010

SEARCHING WITH JOSEPH

On the third day
You found him
'Why have you treated us like this?'
You asked
Exhausted by anxiety.
You were not there
On that other third day
When the Son was missing.
The anxiety was the same;
And so was his answer:
'Do you not understand
That it was necessary
To be on my Father's business?'

2010

THE ROSE BUD

Nearing death,
Your memory gives birth
To a vision of
Long forgotten tenderness.
An old farm worker
Taking a rose bud
To his dying wife,
And showing her
Its bright dew-wet
Bursting bud of colour.
You were a
Young doctor then.
Now
You cannot heal yourself,
And your eyes
Are bright wet with tears
For all you will not see.

2010

MY DEAREST WISH[6]

My dearest wish
be Christ-like Christians;
like him,
bow down,
and serve;
seek truth,
simplicity
and love:
in our personal,
touching Lord.

My dearest wish
be Christ-like Christians;
be open;
broken hearted:
Go bravely on
and know
His love
will never let you go.

My dearest wish
be Christ-like Christians;
trust his perfect wisdom;
dwell in his peace
and unity;
hope in Him
our daily
duty.

---

[6] For the centenary of Bishop Edward King

My dearest wish
be Christ-like Christians;
be refreshed by Him;
seek His forgiving grace;
His gentleness
will make us great.

2010

BREAD AND STONES

In the wilderness
Stones could be bread.
If you
Gave the word.
The hard, dry world
Could be filled
With the scent of
Warm dough
And a freshness
Enlivening
Every sense.

You said
No:

The world remained
Hard baked
And half dead
Until
At the end
You turned your body
Into bread
To feed the hungry
To eternity.

2010

HOPE IS A DUTY

Hammer Hope.
My hope hammer
fear out. Hope
hammer out
this want of
love in me.

Drive it home
Drive in Faith
nail my will
on you alone.
Fix me on the
tree of life.

Fix me on
your life. Fix
your truth
on me. Hold
me down and
then I will
be free.

2010

THE SERAPHIM OF EZEKIEL

Wonderful and six-winged
borne on wheels of fire,
eternally fixed on their maker's desire.

At creation's heart,
there life is simple being:
free by serving and wise by seeing.

Source of all song unheard and unsung;
first work of the Father
when creation was young.

In ceaseless ecstasy
of closeness to Him;
whose throne is the stars,
and whose crown is the sun.

2011

PRAYER TO A GUARDIAN ANGEL

Come in the night
Silent and still,
Angel of light
show the truth of love's will.
Dark is my soul
And fearful my mind:
Help me the purest
and gentlest way find.

Come in the dawn
When all is lost,
Angel of comfort
Take hold of my hand.
Lift me, enfold me,
Help me to see
That all of your treasures
give power to break free.

Come in the noon
Of bright sunlit days;
Angel of joy
Give me right words to say.
Inspire my heart
with truth from above;
Renew my life in the healing
of perfect love.

2011

THE LAST LULLABY

Go to sleep now O true love of mine,
Hold in your heart the comfort Divine;
Angels above you
Guard you and watch you,
Sleepless their vigil can never tire.

With all your memory cherish today,
All we have shared each life-long day:
Angels of light will
scatter the darkness
Tenderly lifting the weight of pain.

You have I loved since we were so young,
With you I sang each beautiful song;
Angels of life
O Give me your voice,
Help me to sing our last lullaby.

2012

THE ARCHANGEL SUITE

I. MICHAEL

Almighty Michael,
All present guard of goodness;
Love's protector
Truth's defender:
Bearer of the sword of light.

Be our defender!
Be our protector!
Prince of all the host of heaven
Save us in this time of danger!

Purest beauty,
Sweetest music;
Faith; Hope; Love:
The armour of God.

His strong defender,
His present hope in danger!
I am his sword!
I am his slayer!
Victor of the heights of heaven!

Almighty Michael!
Our present guard of goodness,
Confound the devil!
You are his slayer!

Michael, the glorious victor!
Lord of the hosts of angels!
Always faithful!
Always fearless!
Blessed Michael,
Lead our praises.

All heaven praise Him!
All earth laud Him!
May His kingdom come on earth!
The kingdom of Christ!

Blessing and honour and glory and power,
Be yours for ever and ever! Amen!

2012

II. RAPHAEL

Raphael,
Chosen,
Most trusted.

Tender healer,
Gentle saver,
Watcher,
Hear us.

Save us!
Heal us!
Hold us!
Surround us!
Look down:
Renew us!

2012

III. GABRIEL

Hear the herald of God's new age,
Hear the hope of good news,
Hear the name above every name,
This name, the prince of all names.

Hear the name of Jesus,
Saviour of the world,
Come and with your hearts and lips adore.

Sweetest Lady, Hear the Word.
Highly favoured, full of grace and love.
A sword will pierce
your own heart and soul,
Your journey will be alone:
You will part in the dark of noon
And by the cold of a tomb.

Then your child shall rise again
And empty will be the tomb.
Jesus is the hope of every dawn.

At his name all knees shall bow
And confess Him King of Glory now.

Hear the herald.
Hear the hope of good news.

2012

IV. URIEL

I gaze on His face,
I see in His eyes;
With the south wind
I come
from His side.

South wind bring you home,
Come with strength and love:
Messenger of hope
From God above.

Not the broken reed,
Nor the flickering flame,
Will break, nor die,
Within my hands.

When faith is new born,
And our doubt profound,
And we fear the loss of all,
Source of comfort
Hear our call.

I will bring you strength,
I will bring you light:
I will guide you
In your darkest night.

2012

BLOOD AND WATER[7]

We share the same blood
As my grandfathers;
One who wore clogs
On the fish dock;
One who ruined by war
Made life simple and quiet.
There are certain things
I might hand on:
You might keep your left hand in your pocket
Whenever you use your right hand to pour tea;
You might be left handed
Or have problems spelling.
But, in our case, water
Is thicker than blood.
It is water from the side of Jesus,
Water mixed in his cup.
It hands on life
And hope
Beyond all living and dying.
Your memory of me may die
(I can only just hear my grandfather's Welsh
        accent).
But the mark Christ made on you
Through me
Is a promise of eternity.

2012

---

[7] On the baptism of grandson Rufus

THE DYING TREE

Without anyone noticing
The ancient yew
Is dying
Of thirst.

All pass by
As the drought
Crucifies
This sign of eternity
Rooted among
The graves.

The church
Over looks
This slow public death;
Fearing
That
One day
It too might perish
From neglect.

2012

DIVES AND LAZARUS

At a Lenten Eucharist,
There was priest
Dressed in
Purple and fine linen,
Who feasted
Sumptuously
On the Bread of Life.
Inside
His heart
Lay a poor man,
Full of sores
Desiring to be fed
Only on fallen
Scraps.
In the presence of
God,
A fire burns
Between them,
Purifying, life-giving,
Eternal.
Evidence of the
One
Who has risen from the dead.

2012

GUILE

Dear God
I would like
To be
Without
Guile.

Guile is a
Horrid
Thick skin,
It is a
Piercing eye
That sees
The fault-line
In every
Thing.

It affords grace
To oil through
Life
Without banging
And scraping on
Awkward truths.

It is necessary
To survive.
But
Will not help
Me thrive.

2012

SNOW AND SIN

Lord do not spread a
Gentle blanket of snow
On my heart.
It burns with such strong
Wrong desire
- That it will surely disappear
Like the morning dew.
Thrash it with hail,
Penetrate it with
A chilling frost;
Compel its deviance to still
And die.

2012

NOT A FAIRY TALE

Seeking solace
Wondering
About the way.
Taking the path
By the monastery garth
To the deep still pool.

One white feather
Fell
Swooping and halting.

A thought of angels
Announced itself.

Could I believe the sign?
Or
Was it a sign
That they believed in me?

2012

NEW FIRE

Fire.
Light
Of Christ
Floods
Over all.

Catching
Each by name.

Together
We are
Fire.

2013

FALLEN OFF

We have fallen off
The shoulders of giants.
Or
Were we pushed?
Now we are stuck in the mire:
Levelled by that great god
Equality.

Pride came before
The fall.
There was necessary humility
In standing on others:
Seeing
Through their eyes.
Without true vision
We perish.

Where do we start from here;
This place of insecurity and fear?

2014

OUTSTANDING[8]

Is standing outside
With a child
Who is frightened to come in:
Coming in with a child
Who is difficult in the class:
The class that demands the
Most individual of guidance:
Guidance that takes every
Ounce of patience
And preparation:
Preparation that means going
To the limit of what is known:
What is known is
That this child is very sad:
The school is sad because he cannot stay.
He will always stand outside.
Can we be outstanding?

2014

---

[8] For the staff of Edenham School with deference to
OFSTED.

WIZ

In troubled sleep
You bounded towards me,
That question mark tail
Wagging you.
I was thrilled
To see you
Old friend:
Companion of our young family
Our co-adventurer
And comforter
Out of the peaceful past.
You came:
I put out my hand
And you bit it
Drawing blood.
I woke up in pain;
Resolving
To put you down.

2014

THE ANGEL OF MONS

I. FOR KING AND COUNTRY

Long expected; well prepared;
The militia men are gathering.
In every town, on every green
The yeomanry are mustering.

Ploughmen, thatchers, clerks and smiths
Their daily task relinquishing,
Are encamped throughout the land
In deadly earnest practicing.

Volunteers by veterans led
Are off to fight heroically,
Their hearts of oak, their honest wills
To God and right entrusting.

Down Jack-dressed streets
Through cheering crowds they're marching.
As England's white cliffs sail from sight
The adventure is beginning.

2014

II. THE MARCH TO MONS

Long roads and heavy loads
Silence to song.
New boots and August's heat
Wound their feet.
Each long day the enemy
draws near,
Each short night darkens
In private fears.

Into an unknown land the
Little army comes;
Driven by the desire that
Duty's done.
In chaotic mystery the opening
Scenes unfold.
In pain and blood the first
Reports are told.

Black storm clouds hide the living
Light of sun;
Broken scattered, leaderless and lost
In God they trust.
Night time thunder mingles with the guns;
And lightning strikes like terror
On the men.

2014

CHRISTMAS POEMS

CHRISTMAS EVE SEQUENCE[9]

I.   WE WILL MAKE OUR CRIB

Tonight we make our Christmas Crib,
Tonight we hear again
how Jesus was born in a stable bare –
to bring God's love to all men.

Tonight we make our Christmas Crib,
to remind us of all that took place –
and in our hearts on this Holy night
is no distance in time or space.

Tonight we make our Christmas Crib,
and in each figure we will see,
how the folk who welcomed Jesus
were people like you and me.

Tonight we make our Christmas Crib,
Tonight we remember with joy,
and the carols we sing
will make heaven ring
with the love that we give Mary's boy.

1986

---

[9] For Gedney Drove End Sunday School

II. THE ANIMALS IN THE STABLE

Jesus was born in a stable,
not a house or a hospital ward.
There, far from home, in the noise and the
    gloom
the light of the world sleeps in straw.

The creatures His Heavenly Father
had made with such beauty and care,
were the first to adore the Lord Jesus –
the creator asleep in their stall.

Why Jesus was born in a stable,
is a lesson that has to be learnt;
- it is that we and all creatures -
should live in God's peace on His earth.

1986

III. THE SHEPHERDS

It was not the clever or wealthy,
it was not the famous or wise,
that God called to greet the Lord Jesus;
to see how His promise arrived.

It was men working in silence,
alone, in the dark, on a hill;
men whose work was not clean and not nice,
(there are plenty who live like that still).

But to them all God's Angels sang welcome,
it was they who first heard the good news;
and the heavenly lights that shone all around,
sent them hurrying down the hill.

So let us see men as God sees them,
and when we ask – "What is he worth?"
remember it was first the poorest,
who came to our Lord, at His birth.

1986

IV. THE WISE MEN

The Wise Men were ever so clever,
at the seeing of signs in the stars;
at reading the oldest of stories,
in languages terribly hard.

But, they could not find the Lord Jesus,
by sitting alone in their room,
but by making a journey together;
and leaving their library at home.

For all truth can only find meaning,
and meaning's real growth in us start,
when we put our minds where love is,
and learn all God's lessons by heart.

The Wise Men they found the Lord Jesus,
and in looking they found their true selves;
for Jesus call all of us to Him,
that we might know all truth as well.

1986

THE JESSE TREE

I. THE EDEN CAROL

When out of the ground Adam was made,
and from his rib was built a maid;
then God saw that all was good
and set them in the garden glade.

He gave them each and every flower,
He gave them ev'ry fruit-filled bower,
and in the midst he set a tree;
its fruit made man like God to see.

And so a tree begins it all;
a tree, it was, that caused the fall;
the snake did ask the question deep;
Did Adam and Eve all knowledge seek?

Such knowledge deep they could not bear,
their hearts were broke beyond repair,
their friendship with the land was gone,
for peace and hope their being longed.

And so the Lord re-worked His plan
to recreate the heart of man;
from deepest dark of hidden love
with farthest light of star above.

So God's plan a new start makes
when God's love all chances take.
The tree new-set all barren stands
Its fruit decays in Adam's hand.   *1993*

II. THE ARK CAROL

The rain it drops, drips, drops and runs
down mountainsides, through canyons;
the floods arise and drown the trees
a baptism of all that breathes.
In Noah's Ark the whole world floats,
the kangaroos and long-haired goats.
The tree-trunk keel skims mountain heights,
the tree-trunk mast the black sky spikes.

By surging tides, by swirling winds,
the Lord is cleansing everything.
A new beginning He will make
to all that's wrecked by Adam's snake.
Full forty days of purging rain
to purify the deepest stain.
Full forty nights of drumming drops,
at last the purgatory stops.

Now Noah looks for signs of peace;
a dove returns with olive leaves!
And so a tree takes up the tale;
from deep water a new world sails!
And in the sky a rainbow shines,
God's promise is to last all time!
The world will in each season stand
until He shapes the end of man.

1993

III. ABRAHAM'S CAROL

In the soft shade of Mamre trees
my tents are pitched, my flocks roam free.
I journey far from my own land
led by God Almighty's hand.

And as I rest in noonday's heat,
I see three men come close to meet;
I bow low in their presence great
and bid them visit my retreat.

They around my table sit,
I offer them my best as gift;
they in return a promise make,
God will from me a nation make.

From my body old and dry
He will raise His chosen tribe.
To the land of promise I will go,
where milk and honey richly flow.

In the soft shade of Mamre trees
my tents are pitched, my flocks roam free.
The Trinity has been my guest
and stirred me from my waiting rest.

1993

IV. JESSE'S CAROL

When Samuel the prophet came
and bid me – "Call your sons by name!"
I did not dream; I could not know;
What wonders waited to unfold.

With all my sons he stood and prayed
and then, at last, the youngest bade,
and in the sheepfold he was sought
and to the seer was swiftly brought.

In an eye's wink all things were changed;
"He is the one, the Lord has claimed!"
This shoot of mine was to be king,
peace, hope and riches he would bring.

Of making war, he did not tire,
breaking God's foes by blade and fire.
In making music and in dance
he praised our Lord and gave Him thanks.

And now, I trust, the saying's true;
from my old stump new life will shoot,
and there will come another king,
to uphold truth; God's kingdom bring.

1993

158

V. ISAIAH'S CAROL

He gave me eyes into His heart,
He gave me strength to bear His part,
He gave my mind far-seeing sight,
to bring me to a dark land light.

The day that king Uzziah died,
I saw the Lord uplifted high,
with hot fire he touched my speech;
he sent me out; "My message teach!"
The message that he lay on me
was one of hope and charity;
He gave the sign "Emmanuel";
he sent me out; "His meaning spell!"

He gave me eyes into His heart,
He gave me strength to bear His part,
He gave my mind far-seeing sight,
to bring me to a dark land light.

Emmanuel is pure-virgin born;
"God-with-us" – a new-world's dawn;
Wonderful Counsellor, prince of peace,
the flowering of the Jesse Tree.
Despised and rejected is His fate
but by His death God's love will take –
and shoot and root into man's soul
and heal the wounds so deep and cold.

He gave me eyes into His heart,
He gave me strength to bear His part,
He gave my mind far-seeing sight,
to bring me to a dark land light.   *1993*

159

VI. THE BAPTIST'S CAROL

In the treeless
desert place,
I lift my voice
your world to shake!

Spin your life round!
Reject the wrong!
Turn to the Lord!
Make Him your song!

Remake your way!
Just spend your pay!
Do not cheat!
All the low keep!

For He will come!
God's will be done!
Put to the fire!
Each wrong desire!

God will forgive!
If you repent!
Listen to me!
For I am sent!

1993

VII. THE CROSS CAROL

The ancient stories, I've heard say,
"The cross it stood on Adam's grave";
that "the cruel branches of the rood
were Eden's trees long-seasoned wood".

Jesus, the Son of Joseph knew
the power in a woodman's tools.
To rid the world of darkest night,
He reshaped the Tree of Life.

By three nails, two planks of wood,
He made a ladder true and good
He climbed deep down to break death's door,
He then rose up life to restore.

1993

JOSEPH'S CAROL

O child that lies soft-
sleeping in my arms,
I shall keep you safe
from all that harms.
I know that your life
did not spring from mine;
and yet I know that
all I am is thine.

My craft is hewing,
joining, making good;
and now my end is
shaped and made by God.
A simple carpenter
my chosen trade;
and now my life is fixed
by powers that all things made.

Your being fulfils
a promise borne of dreams;
both innocence and fear
shall make my destiny.
By starlit night
your midwife I have been.
Your blood on my hands
the offering seals.

O child that lies soft-
sleeping in my arms,
I shall keep you safe
from all that harms.
I know that your life
did not spring from mine;
and yet I know that
all I am is thine.

1996

THE KING'S CAROL

Behold The King!
Bidden by a king,
borne on an ass by a young virgin.
Born a King, His Kingdom to bring.

Behold The King!
His court a stable in an inn,
wakeful animals His praises sing.
Born a King, His peace to bring.

Behold The King!
Enthroned in straw
who frightened shepherds first adored.
Born a King, new hope to bring.

Behold The King!
His mother a Queen
robed in grace – full poverty.
Born a King, Love to bring.

Behold our King
and God and sing
of His majestic emptying!
Born with nothing His kingdom to bring.

1997

MIDNIGHT MASS

In muted light we wait:
candles whisper in murmuring reflections.
"Light from light," we carol –
yet welcome you in shadows.

Was the Blessed's womb tomb-dark?
Were your swaddling clothes transfigured?
In birth your fire was restrained;
withholding flame from the manger's straw.

Yet, there was light that night –
in earth and in the heavens;
a new star blazing a way; and
shepherds dazzled by the glorious news.

Tonight, when my hands cradle you;
presuming your promise of communion,
come Lord, scatter my darkness of heart
- for in your light I shall see light.

1999

MILLENNIAL MOMENTS

Broadcast
by satellite,
the faces of
the shining ones
fly;
at midnight's chime.
Celebrants
of a minutely crafted
festival of time;
The 'history-makers'
are making
scenes for history.

In a distant
star-lit space
a bloodied-baby's
cry
Is soothed in
virginal embrace.
A word is spoken
to the heart of man.
Time has not forgot;
And
Never can.

1999

NATIVITY PLAY

Dressing-gowned shepherds in tea-towel hats;
Magi bear bric-a-brac crowned with cake
    wrap;
Turkey-foiled angels and a tinsel-clad star,
Lead a pantomime donkey on a journey so far.

Joseph blushes red by his blue and white bride,
Who squeezes the baby doll tight, at his side;
The jovial innkeepers bellow their lines –
"We've got no room here!" Till one shouts –
    "try mine!"

The stage is now crowded, the scene is
    complete
"Away in a manger" and "little one sleep";
The Heavenly Father with grans, mums and
    dads
Delights in the singing: it makes His heart glad.

2001

CHRISTMAS CHILDREN

There are few 'grown-ups'
on Christmas Eve:
the shimmering light,
the star-crowned tree,
the greetings and
that sense of safe and warm
can unlock the child
within us all.

We children are
ordained to be:
guardians of a mystery,
partakers of pure gift,
singers of innocency;
watchers in this quiet night
of God revealed
in infancy.

2002

CHRIST THE GIFT

A gift is not a gift
until it is received:
the giver of the gift
must be accepted and believed.

Mary (the most-gifted)
when chosen to conceive
the Gift of Christ The Giver,
could not first believe.

Gabriel, for her comfort,
said "All this will be done;
for God the Heavenly Father
will give the world His Son."

Mary, wondered in herself –
"How might this come to be?"
"His Spirit will overshadow you
and help you to receive."

"For Elizabeth, your cousin,
beyond all natural means
is gifted with a son
that God helped her to conceive."

"Let it be," said Mary,
her being filled with joy;
"I am willing to receive
God's gift of His boy."

God give to me the gift
like Mary to receive,
and in the love of Jesus
to trust, live and believe.

Amen.

2004

O LAMB OF GOD

O Lamb of God, the new born Lord,
who poor shepherds first adored;
it was within your gracious plan
that first to shepherds angels sang.

O Lamb of God, the shepherds gave
the meaning of the life that saves:
for you were born to share our lot;
to know and be known by your flock.

O Lamb of God, pure truth and love,
all your life was Holy, Good;
for you would the Good Shepherd be –
who lays His dear life down for me.

O Lamb of God, my shepherd Lord
who poor shepherds first adored;
you lead me by the living stream
through death's dark vale to pools of peace.

2005

THE COLOURS OF CHRISTMAS

Take gold for the angel wings
and green for the tree
more gold for the star
that all wise men seek.

Take a rainbow of colours –
take red, green and gold:
in the colours of Christmas
a story is told.

Take silver for the moonlight
silent and still,
and red for the firelight
of shepherds on the hill.

Take a rainbow of colours –
take silver, red and blue:
in the colours of Christmas
the story is made true.

Take blue for the Virgin
so loving and pure,
and gold for the straw
on the dark stable floor.

Take white for the bands
that clothe the new king –
the sweet prince of peace
for all angels sing.

Take gold for the angel wings
and green for the tree
more gold for the star
that all wise men seek.

Take a rainbow of colours –
take red, gold and white,
in the colours of Christmas
all darkness turns to light.

2006

FAMILY CHRISTMAS

On dark mid winter's starlit shining roads,
Midnight streetlights kindle dreams of home.
Plane flight, train ride and a heavy load,
In crowds of strangers – a long way to go.
From distant towns we gather once again,
To unpack dreams our longings and our fears;
To the sheltered garden of Church Lane;
A home of laughter, chatter, jokes and tears.
Death may diminish and young love increase;
Life in a family is all chance and change;
Our simple being creates joy and peace.
By partaking small things strength is gained.
We do not only look for bed and board,
But a Christ-like sharing of His Life and Word.

2007

NEW BORN

Herod's soldiers will smash the locks
in streets where Joseph knocked.
The pastures that watched shepherds dream
will shudder as the mothers scream.

From this air of fear-filled death
the new born boy takes His first breath.
Into a world devoid of peace
the Word Eternal comes to speak.

His birth-life-death no favours take,
for Love in Him a hard road makes;
from betrayer's kiss to noon-black fear –
all witnessed by His mother's tears.

This is the Way to our New Birth;
the first dawn of this universe:
the grace-full hope of truth and light
as angels told on Christmas night.

2008

MARANATHA –
COME LORD JESUS

Lord, come to the
unexpecting;
break in and steal
their hearts and will;
surprise them with the light of heaven;
like the shepherds on the hill.

Lord, come to all
thoughtful seekers;
reveal, inspire,
stir up their minds;
lead them, draw them, to your presence
as the Magi came to find.

Lord, come make known
your love and mercy
to all broken homes and lives;
may we, by faith,
with joy receive you;
friend and brother, Love divine.

2009

PRINCE OF PEACE

"Strange peace maker," the doubters say
"He's helpless, sound asleep in hay.
Strange Prince of Peace without a throne
No title or treasure and far from home."

"Strange Lord and King," the doubters say;
"No robes, no be-jeweled signet ring,
Without a crown, not lifted up,
No feasting place or golden cup."

"His peace will reign," my faith replies,
"In Him eternity redeems time.
His peace defies the power of steel;
His life your fear of death can heal."

2010

MARY'S PRAYER

Now we are both alone,
I will stand near;
help me to love you
and live without fear.

Help me to love you
and live without fear;
for the dark and the danger
shall surely draw near.

The dark and the danger
shall surely draw near;
fill me with love that
will cast out all fear.

Fill me with love that
will cast out all fear;
love's light shall keep us
'till the new day appears.

2011

THE HEART OF MARY

Ponder the treasure, in your heart:
Gabriel's message; the glorious dark;
the dangerous road and Joseph's care;
the magi's star; the shepherds' prayer.

Ponder the treasure in your heart:
Simeon's promise at the start of
what will prove your wounded way
by a piercing sword of a noon dark day.

Ponder the treasure in your heart:
the empty tomb; the Pentecost spark;
the spiritual fire that catches light
in all baptized by your Son's life.

Ponder the treasure in your heart:
still full of grace you take your part,
as heavenly Mother, source of prayer
for all who seek God's tender care.

2011

HOW CAN I WRAP HIM?

How can I wrap him,
my little child –
wrap him to warm him
and keep him from harm?

I wrap him in cloths
all clean and white;
to keep out the cold
of the dark of the night.

When he grows up
he will stretch out his arms
to show us his love
that keeps us from harm.

We will wrap him in cloths
all clean and white;
for the cold of his grave;
in the dark of the night.

But cloths will not hold him
he will burst from his grave:
wrapped up in his love
we all will be saved.

2012

THE NATIVITY NAMES
(as found in the first chapter of Luke)

Unbidden and silent came *One God made
    strong,*
Delivering names of two sons, yet unborn.
The Lord Remembers in prayer at God's altar
    stood.
The Angel assured him God's purpose was
    good.

'To *My God is the Faithful One* a boy will be
    born,
A sign for his people – to herald the dawn:
God's Gracious Gift is his given name
He will quicken their hearts to Love's purpose
    again.'

He will be The Forerunner, faithful and strong,
In the way of Elijah he shall confront all wrong.
His name will be known as the world's greatest
    son;
He will straighten the way for the one that will
    come.

In the sixth month *The Strong One* to a Virgin
    appeared:
His coming and message filled her with fear.
'*Perfect One* you are favoured, of all women
    blessed.
God's Son will be born and will be fed at your
    breast.'

His name shall be – *The Lord God Saves*,
This name will be great and the source of all
    praise.
He will reign in a kingdom that will not pass
    away;
All the prophets of old looked in hope for His
    Day.

The *One Who is Perfect* asked, 'how will this
    be?'
'By God's shadowing spirit,' *The Strong One*
    did say.
'For *God is The Faithful One* has conceived a
    son
For no hope is impossible where God's will is
    done.'

2013

A CRIB CAROL

Jesus our King
where is your crown?
Wrapped in poor clothes
in a manger laid down.

Jesus our Lord
where do you reign?
Where is the kingdom
that you came to claim?

Our love is your crown,
our hearts are your throne,
we welcome you Lord
to reign in our homes.

Jesus our brother
please show us the way
to live with Our Father
each step of life's way.

2013

THE STABLE CAROL

Our Little One sleeps in his manger of wood,
Our Lady still ponders the workings of God,
Joseph the Carpenter is silent in awe
as shepherds and magi bow low and adore.

What a strange place for the strangest of births!
The Maker of all has come down to His earth.
From dust unto dust we all have to turn
'til from this small child the new way we learn.

What a wonderful shoot from the old Jesse
    Tree,
What a beautiful fruit the new Eve did
    conceive!
By her simple 'yes' she unlocked the gate
which Eve's greedy eyes had closed in our
    face.

Our Little One sleeps in his manger of wood,
Our Lady still ponders the workings of God,
already the promise of His love is found
where the roots of the True Vine break open
    new ground.

2014

184

LITTLE ONES

You are His little ones – never despair;
He holds you gently in His tender care;
He is the little one laid in the straw
He is the baby poor shepherds adore.

He is our great God who came to his own,
the maker of all things in a manger enthroned.
Not dressed in velvet, but wrapped up in rags
sharing the needs of the lost and the sad.

You are His little ones – never despair;
He holds you gently in His tender care;
each little trouble that worries your mind
will in His love's wisdom the true answer find.

2014

THE CHRISTMAS GOSPEL
(John 1: 1-14)

The Word that did in flesh abide
First proclaimed the light to shine.

The Christ that water turned to wine
Did second say that heaven should rise.

The Word that third made earth for seed
Did by the pool the lame man heal.

The Christ whose blessing bread supplied
Did fourth place stars across the sky.

The Word that fifth filled seas with life
Did enfleshed give blind men sight.

The Christ who ordered Lazarus rise
Did sixth all life on earth provide.

The Word that gave humanity being
Upon the cross made its redeeming.

The Word that did the seventh day rest
In Christ lay in cold linen dressed.
On the eight day the Word did wake
The whole creation to remake.

2014

CHRISTMAS EVE CAROLS

Tonight we are what we used to be;
Gathered together – community.
Tonight we recall words the Psalmist tells
'It is gracious and lovely in union to dwell'.

Tonight in this hour we sing from the heart;
We are one in voice and each bears a part
By the youngest to oldest the story is heard:
The manger, the shepherds, the starlight, we
   share.

Tonight in God's house we forget what we are;
That from one song and story we have travelled
   too far.
We forget all the times we reject all that God's
   giving
And ignore one another in the frenzy of living.

Tonight we are what we used to be;
A people in search of eternity.
Let us pray to the Child Divine
To bring us home to our rightful mind.

2014

THANKS AND ACKNOWLEDGEMENTS

This collection of poems would not exist without the perennial help and encouragement of my wife Siân and my brother Patrick who both believed that I had something to say in poetry when I did not myself. It would certainly not exist without the sacrificial efforts of Andy Berry who took boxes and folders of manuscripts and created order out of chaos.

His work has made me review my poetry and made it possible for me to create something quite beyond my own capabilities.

ANDREW HAWES
2014

INDEX OF TITLES

194